TOEFL Listening Practice Tests: TOEFL Listening Preparation for the Internet-based and Paper Delivered Tests

TOEFL® and TOEFL iBT® are registered trademarks of Educational Testing Service (ETS). This publication is not associated with or endorsed by ETS.

TOEFL Listening Practice Tests: TOEFL Listening Preparation for the Internet-based and Paper Delivered Tests

© COPYRIGHT 2018. Exam SAM Study Aids and Media. www.examsam.com

All rights reserved. No part of this publication may be reproduced, stored in a retrieval system, or transmitted, in any form or by any means, electronic, mechanical, photocopying, recording or otherwise.

TOEFL® and TOEFL iBT® are registered trademarks of Educational Testing Service (ETS). This publication is not associated with or endorsed by ETS.

TABLE OF CONTENTS

TOEFL Listening Test Format	1
How to Use This Publication	2
TOEFL Listening Exam Question Types	3

TOEFL Listening Practice Test 1:

Listening Test 1 – Task 1	5
Listening Test 1 – Task 2	8
Listening Test 1 – Task 3	11
Listening Test 1 – Task 4	15
Listening Test 1 – Task 5	17
Listening Test 1 – Task 6	19
Listening Test 1 – Answer Key	22
Listening Test 1 – Answers and Explanations	23

Listening Test 1 – Texts:

Listening Test 1 – Text 1	29
Listening Test 1 – Text 2	32
Listening Test 1 – Text 3	35
Listening Test 1 – Text 4	38
Listening Test 1 – Text 5	40
Listening Test 1 – Text 6	43

TOEFL Listening Practice Test 2:

Listening Test 2 – Task 1 ... 47

Listening Test 2 – Task 2 ... 49

Listening Test 2 – Task 3 ... 51

Listening Test 2 – Task 4 ... 54

Listening Test 2 – Task 5 ... 56

Listening Test 2 – Task 6 ... 58

Listening Test 2 – Answer Key ... 60

Listening Test 2 – Answers and Explanations ... 61

Listening Test 2 – Texts:

Listening Test 2 – Text 1 ... 68

Listening Test 2 – Text 2 ... 71

Listening Test 2 – Text 3 ... 74

Listening Test 2 – Text 4 ... 77

Listening Test 2 – Text 5 ... 79

Listening Test 2 – Text 6 ... 82

TOEFL Listening Practice Test 3:

Listening Test 3 – Task 1 ... 84

Listening Test 3 – Task 2 ... 86

Listening Test 3 – Task 3 ... 88

Listening Test 3 – Task 4 ... 91

Listening Test 3 – Task 5 93

Listening Test 3 – Task 6 95

Listening Test 3 – Answer Key 97

Listening Test 3 – Answers and Explanations 98

Listening Test 3 – Texts:

Listening Test 3 – Text 1 105

Listening Test 3 – Text 2 107

Listening Test 3 – Text 3 110

Listening Test 3 – Text 4 114

Listening Test 3 – Text 5 116

Listening Test 3 – Text 6 119

TOEFL Listening Test Format

Before you begin the TOEFL iBT listening test, you will be asked to put on a set of headphones. You will have the opportunity to adjust the volume on your computer before the listening test starts. You may see different photos of people on the screen at the beginning of each section as you take the iBT listening test. The photos may help you understand the situation or context of the conversation that you are going to hear.

For both the iBT and paper-delivered tests, you will hear conversations, class discussions, and lectures in the listening test. You should take notes as you listen to each task.

For the internet-based test, individual questions will appear on your screen after each recording has finished based on what you have just heard. You will need to click on the "Next" and "OK" buttons on your screen after you answer each question

For the paper based test, you will need to answer the questions in your test booklet when the examiner indicates that you may do so.

How to Use This Publication

To simulate the real exam, you should not read the questions before you hear the recording. You should listen to each recording only once, taking notes as you listen. After you have listened to each task, use your notes to answer the questions. Then go to the next task.

Links to the mp3 listening files for this publication can be found at:

www.examsam.com/toefl-ibt/listening/

TOEFL Listening Test Question Types

There are seven different types of questions on the TOEFL listening test.

1. Identifying the main idea – For recordings of academic lectures, you will have to identify the main idea from the answer choices provided.

2. Understanding specific details – For all of the types of recordings, you will be asked about certain excerpts of the conversation or lecture and will need to demonstrate that you have understood certain specific points.

3. Making an inference – For this type of question, the information you need for your answer is not stated directly in the recording. Rather, you will have to draw a conclusion based the information stated in the recording.

4. Understanding implications – The information you need to answer this type of question is also not directly stated in the recording. Rather, you will have to decide what is implied by the information stated in the recording.

5. Summarizing key points – You will see answer choices that contain summaries, and you will have to choose the best group of statements.

6. Understanding idioms – idioms are expressions that do not have a literal meaning. If you do not know the idiom, you may be able to make a reasonable guess based on the context of the recording.

7. Understanding rhetorical function – These types of questions will ask you why a speaker used a certain phrase or how a speaker has supported his or her argument.

TOEFL Listening Practice Test 1

This listening practice test contains 6 parts (34 total questions). You have 60 minutes to complete all six parts of this listening test.

Listening Test 1 – Task 1:

1. What does the student mean when he says this?

    "A problem is more like it!"

    A. He wants to reiterate that he is not responsible for causing the problem.

    B. He wants to clear up a misunderstanding he has had with the accommodation office.

    C. He is entreating the accommodation officer to deal with his case leniently.

    D. He is trying to emphasize that his situation may be more problematic than the ones the accommodation office usually addresses.

2. According to the member of staff, when do accommodation transfers normally take place?

    A. At the beginning of a semester

    B. In the middle of a semester

C. At the end of a semester

D. Only when there are extenuating circumstances.

3. Why does the student want to change his accommodation?

   A. His room does not have laptop facilities.

   B. He has had a dispute with the Resident Director.

   C. The accommodation is too far from the library.

   D. The residence hall is too noisy, and he cannot study there.

4. What is the member of staff implying when she says this?

   "I'm surprised you weren't introduced to him during your student orientation."

   A. The sole purpose of the student orientation is to introduce the Resident Director.

   B. Students are introduced to their Resident Director as an integral part of the orientation program.

   C. The member of staff finds the student's revelation shocking and upsetting.

   D. The member of staff thinks that the student has lied to her.

5. What is the outcome at the end of this conversation?

   A. The Resident Director will warn the noisy students.

   B. The accommodation office will transfer the student to another room.

   C. The student has agreed to speak with his Resident Director about the problem.

   D. The student will try to study in his room during study hours.

Listening Test 1 – Task 2:

6. What is the main idea of the lecture?

   A. Different types of educational strategies

   B. The variety of assessment models available to teachers

   C. The specific aspects of the student readiness model

   D. The disadvantages of the question adjustment method

7. What does the professor imply when she says this?

   It goes without saying that I hope everyone has read the background reading for today!

   A. The students should have done the reading.

   B. The reading for the class was arduous.

   C. She hopes the class will enjoy the discussion.

   D. She realizes that several students are not prepared.

8. How does the professor support her statement that "student readiness is not a static entity"?

   A. By mentioning that some students have a "comfort zone"

   B. By discussing the needs of above-average students

   C. By explaining the ways in which a student's level can change

   D. By citing data and statistics

9. What does the professor state about curriculum design?

   A. It is the duty of the teacher to decide which design is best.

   B. Teachers usually disagree about the curriculum.

   C. Question adjustment often thwarts curriculum design.

   D. It is especially important for below-average students.

10. Which one of the following is the best description of the "question adjustment" strategy?

    A. The teacher's questions should exceed the students' level in order to challenge all of the students.

    B. The teacher should ask mainly easy questions to build student confidence.

    C. The teacher should ask questions at various levels of difficulty.

    D. The teacher should ask each individual student a different question.

11. Which one of the following statements is correct according to the discussion?

   A. Students prefer informal assessment.

   B. Students will only be confident when they have a high level of readiness.

   C. Posters are generally more effective for more advanced students.

   D. Formal assessments are used to determine a student's grade for a course.

Listening Test 1 – Task 3:

12. What is the main idea of this lecture?

    A. To elaborate on the construction methods for buildings around the world.

    B. To enumerate the problems encountered in the construction of the HSBC building.

    C. To show how the HSBC building project illustrates construction in urban areas that have limited space.

    D. To criticize the effect that the HSBC construction project had on the environment.

13. How does the professor support his statement that the HSBC building project was "a truly international effort"?

    A. By mentioning where the building was erected.

    B. By giving further details about local geology.

    C. By demonstrating that the employees on the project came from various countries.

    D. By discussing where various pre-manufactured components of the building were made.

14. Based on the lecture, what can be inferred about the basement of the HSBC building?

   A. It had to be carefully planned and properly constructed in order to support the significant weight of the structure.

   B. Because it was twelve stories in height, it was much larger than necessary.

   C. Its design was facilitated by the soft ground in the surrounding area.

   D. It brought about the collapse of the entire building.

15. Which of the following statements best describes the eight giant steel columns?

   A. They were easy to support because of their relatively light weight.

   B. They were sunk into the bedrock below the building.

   C. Their erection was impeded by the heavy clay in the trenches.

   D. They were only used on a temporary basis.

16. What does the professor say about the prefabricated elements of the building?

   A. Fortunately, most of the pre-built components were acquired locally.

   B. They caused inconvenience to many people working near the site.

   C. They helped to avert subsidence of the structure.

   D. They were efficacious in this particular construction project.

17. According to the lecture, which of the following groups of statements is completely true?

   A. (i) All of the HSBC structure was built on site.

   (ii) Parts of the building came from Japan.

   (iii) The part of the structure below ground was made waterproof.

   B. (i) Parts of the building came from Japan.

   (ii) The part of the structure below ground was made waterproof.

   (iii) A system of hangers was used to construct each floor.

C. (i) All of the HSBC structure was built on site.

   (ii) The part of the structure below ground was made waterproof.

   (iii) A system of hangers was used to construct each floor.

D. (i) The part of the structure below ground was made waterproof.

   (ii) A system of hangers was used to construct each floor.

   (iii) The external walls were in a contrasting color to the rest of the building.

Listening Test 1 – Task 4:

18. How did Lewis and Clark become friends?

    A. They were neighbors.

    B. They worked in the same branch of the government

    C. They were in the same local division of the army.

    D. They were the same age.

19. Who offered Lewis the job of exploring the west?

    A. Jefferson

    B. Clark

    C. Congress

    D. the army

20. Why did Clark travel with Lewis?

    A. Lewis felt he needed a partner.

    B. Clark felt he needed a partner.

    C. Because of financial restrictions.

    D. Because he did not have the necessary skills himself.

21. Why were Lewis and Clark good as partners?

    A. They each had different personal characteristics.

    B. They were dissimilar in temperament.

    C. They shared many traits and abilities.

    D. They reacted differently to pressure.

22. What happened after the expedition had finished?

    A. Clark died unexpectedly.

    B. The Louisiana Territory was purchased.

    C. The Missouri River was discovered.

    D. President Jefferson passed away.

Listening Test 1 – Task 5:

23. What is the main idea of this discussion?

    A. the discovery of brain waves

    B. the reasons for brain dysfunction

    C. various scans of brain activity

    D. the function of the human brain and how to measure it

24. What was Edgar Adrian's most important discovery?

    A. The heart has electrical activity.

    B. The brain and the heart are similar physiologically.

    C. The brain emits electrical impulses.

    D. Theta waves facilitate other brain waves.

25. Why is the definition of brain death controversial?

    A. Because the purpose of the cerebral cortex is unknown.

    B. Because other parts of the body may function after a person is no longer capable of rational thought.

    C. Because of legal regulations.

    D. Because some people may object to the use of brain scans.

26. What does the student mean when he says this?

    "I'll take a stab at it."

    A. I'm reluctant to do it.

    B. I'll try to do it.

    C. I wish you hadn't asked me.

    D. I have no choice.

27. From the discussion, what can be inferred about PET scans?

    A. They are more or less identical to the CAT scan.

    B. They are superior to the MRI scan.

    C. Patients would probably rather forego PET scans.

    D. They are constantly in high demand.

28. How does the professor support his comments about the indispensability of the MRI scan?

    A. By citing a medical authority

    B. By giving statistical data

    C. By giving an example

    D. By providing a reason

Listening Test 1 – Task 6:

29. What is the main idea of this lecture?

    A. To discuss past and present scientific discoveries in the Antarctic

    B. To give historical information about Antarctic exploration.

    C. To lament the greenhouse effect

    D. To explain the geological phenomena common to Antarctica

30. How does the professor organize her explanation of the earliest expeditions to the Antarctic?

    A. She organizes them in order of their scientific significance.

    B. She gives the information in chronological sequence.

    C. She discusses the United States first of all, and then Britain.

    D. She focuses on discoveries by air, before mentioning the expeditions on land.

31. How does the professor support her claim about the importance of the research conducted in Antarctica?

    A. By providing information about new factual discoveries, including specific measurements

    B. By discussing a common trend

C. By exemplifying a process

D. By identifying the conclusions reached by a famous scientist

32. What causes atrophy of the Antarctic ice sheet?

    A. rain

    B. frost

    C. melting

    D. snowing

33. What is the professor implying when she says this?

    "Unfortunately, both methods have a rather large potential for error."

    A. Neither of the methods should be utilized.

    B. The results from the two methods need to be interpreted carefully.

    C. A new method should be put in place soon.

    D. Each method will overestimate the results.

34. Which of the following groups of statements gives the best summary of the lecture?

    A. (i) Ernest Shackleton was the first to explore Antarctica.

    (ii) There have been several important expeditions to the Antarctic in the twentieth and twenty-first centuries.

(iii) Expeditions to the Antarctic have resulted in many important scientific discoveries.

B. (i) There have been several important expeditions to the Antarctic in the twentieth and twenty-first centuries.

(ii) Expeditions to the Antarctic have resulted in many important scientific discoveries.

(iii) The Antarctic ice sheet constantly shrinks and expands.

C. (i) Expeditions to the Antarctic have resulted in many important scientific discoveries.

(ii) The Antarctic ice sheet constantly shrinks and expands.

(iii) Scientific discoveries about the Antarctic help us to understand the world's ecosphere.

D. (i) There have been several important expeditions to the Antarctic in the twentieth and twenty-first centuries.

(ii) Expeditions to the Antarctic have resulted in many important scientific discoveries.

(iii) Scientific discoveries about the Antarctic help us to understand the world's ecosphere.

Listening Test 1 – Answer Key

1. D
2. A
3. D
4. B
5. C
6. C
7. A
8. C
9. A
10. C
11. D
12. C
13. D
14. A
15. B
16. D
17. B
18. C
19. A
20. A
21. C
22. B
23. D
24. C
25. B
26. B
27. C
28. D
29. A
30. B
31. A
32. C
33. B
34. D

Listening Test 1 – Answers and Explanations

1) The correct answer is D. The student says the above statement in response to "Have you got a question?" So, he is trying to stress that he doesn't have a commonly-asked question, but rather a serious problem.

2) The correct answer is A. The accommodation officer says: "we usually don't consider any accommodation transfers until the beginning of a new semester."

3) The correct answer is D. The student states: "Well, it's really noisy. I can't study in my room."

4) The correct answer is B. By saying that she is surprised, the accommodation officer implies that this is a normal part of the orientation.

5) The correct answer is C. At the end of the conversation, the student remarked: "I'll have a talk with John [the Resident Director]."

6) The correct answer is C. At the beginning of the discussion, the teacher says, "so let's look at the pedagogical approach that we are going to discuss today: the student readiness model."

7) The correct answer is A. "It goes without saying" means that you are expected to have done something, in this case, the reading.

8) The correct answer is C. The teacher explains that "some students will become more confident throughout the semester and will be able to

increase their student readiness, and unfortunately other students may fall behind and might slip to a below-average position."

9) The correct answer is A. The teacher says that "the onus falls on us as teachers . . . to work out how best to design the curriculum." "Onus" means duty or responsibility.

10) The correct answer is C. The student correctly explains that "the teacher will ask questions at a variety of different levels of difficulty."

11) The correct answer is D. The student remarks that "the formal ones are those that count towards the mark or grade for the course, but the informal ones don't."

12) The correct answer is C. At the very beginning of the lecture, the professor states: "This is especially true in the world's most heavily populated cities. No recent construction project exemplifies this more clearly than the building of the Hong Kong and Shanghai Bank Corporation (HSBC)."

13) The correct answer is D. The professor mentions that components were fabricated in Austria, the United States, Japan, and Germany.

14) The correct answer is A. The professor remarks: "For this reason, the disruption of the ground water supply had to be carefully pondered prior to

construction of the HSBC headquarters to ensure that subsidence, and potentially collapse of the structure, could be averted."

15) The correct answer is B. The professor states: "In order to support the weight of the building, deep wells were sunk in the bedrock below the building, and then filled with concrete, to anchor each of the eight steel columns."

16) The correct answer is D. The professor said: "The prefabrication also had the advantage of making the construction more efficient." The words "efficient" and "efficacious" are synonyms.

17) The correct answer is B. The other statements are false according to the speaker.

18) The correct answer is C. Lewis and Clark became friends because they were in the same local division of the army. The speaker states: "The two men met when Lewis joined the local militia."

19) The correct answer is A. Jefferson offered Lewis the job of exploring the west. The speaker explains that "when Lewis was a young captain in the army, he received a letter from Jefferson offering him a job in charge of an expedition to explore the Western country."

20) The correct answer is A. Clark traveled with Lewis because Lewis felt he needed a partner. The lecturer comments that "Lewis told President Jefferson that it would be preferable to have a partner for the rigorous journey westward. With Jefferson's permission, Lewis offered the assignment to his friend Clark."

21) The correct answer is C. Lewis and Clark were good as partners because they shared many traits and abilities. The speaker states: "They both possessed many traits that would prove to be crucial for such a daunting expedition."

22) The correct answer is B. The Louisiana Territory was purchased after the expedition had finished. The speaker says that "when their expedition had safely concluded, President Jefferson purchased the Louisiana Territory."

23) The correct answer is D. At the beginning of the lecture, the professor says: "This afternoon, we'll be looking at the function of the human brain. We will also be talking about the way the function, as well as the dysfunction, of the human brain is measured."

24) The correct answer is C. The professor said: "Edgar Adrian, a Briton, clearly demonstrated that the brain, like the heart, is profuse in its electrical activity."

25) The correct answer is B. The speaker states that "on the other hand, some say that mere damage to the cerebral cortex is not enough. They assert that brain stem function must also cease before a person can be declared dead, because the cerebral cortex is responsible for other bodily processes."

26) The correct answer is B. "Take a stab at" means to attempt something.

27) The correct answer is C. The student explains that "as far as patients are concerned, the CAT is far less invasive [than the PET] because they don't need to ingest a radioactive substance."

28) The correct answer is D. The teacher explains that "the MRI is perhaps the most indispensable of all of the various scans due to its ability to map the brain in three dimensions."

29) The correct answer is A. At the beginning of the lecture, the professor states: "the southernmost continent [Antarctica] has been the source of a great deal of scientific investigation."

30) The correct answer is B. She begins in 1907, then mentions 1908 to 1909, then 1911, 1956, and the present day.

31) The correct answer is A. She discusses the measurement of the ice sheet at great length.

32) The correct answer is C. The professor explains that "this mammoth sheet of ice atrophies because of year-round melting at its base." "Atrophy" means loss of something.

33) The correct answer is B. The phrase "large potential for error" means that the results need to be considered with care.

34) The correct answer is D. These are the main ideas from the lecture. The other statements contain specific points.

Listening Test 1 – Texts

Listening Test 1 – Task 1:

Student: Hi, I was wondering if you could help me.

Staff: Well, I hope so . . . Have you got a question?

Student: Yeah, well, a problem is more like it!

Staff: Oh . . . That doesn't sound too good!

Student: The thing is . . . I'm living in Henderson Hall right now, but I'm wondering if it will be . . . if I could move to a different residential hall. I mean, I want to move immediately, if possible.

Staff: Um, that's kind of an unorthodox request. Not many students request to be moved in the middle of a term. And we usually don't consider any accommodation transfers until the beginning of a new semester, apart from compelling cases.

Student: What do you mean by "compelling cases"?

Staff: It just means that you have to have a really strong reason why you need to move immediately. Is there anything that makes your request to move more urgent?

Student: Well, it's really noisy. I can't study in my room. So I am finding it extremely frustrating . . . if I want to read, or write an essay or something.

Staff: Oh, I'm sorry, but that's just such a common complaint. I mean, we hear it all the time here at the accommodation office. And to be honest, that's why the library is open 24 hours . . . uh . . . we recommend that students study there.

Student: I see where you're going with this . . . It's just that Henderson Hall is quite far from the library. So I have to carry my laptop and all the books there, and of course, then I have to carry them back to my room again, which is very tiring.

Staff: Yes, but the library has a computer lab for students, so you wouldn't necessarily have to take your laptop, would you?

Student: Uh . . . the library has a computer lab . . . that's true . . . but it's usually completely full, and there aren't any free computers available.

Staff: Oh, that is a bit tricky.

Student: And, of course, it's so distracting in my room with all the loud music.

Staff: Have you tried speaking to your Resident Director about it?

Student: What's a "resident director"?

Staff: That's the person who lives in your hall of residence and who's in charge of day-to-day activities there, as well as complaints.

Student: Okay . . . so who's the Resident Director in charge of Henderson Hall?

Staff: Uh . . . let's have a look on my list . . . Let's see . . . here it is . . . It's John Marshall. I'm surprised you weren't introduced to him during your student orientation.

Student: That's my fault, I'm afraid. I missed orientation because I arrived on campus late. So we were never introduced.

Staff: Okay, well . . . that certainly clears up the mystery! I'd suggest that you have a talk with John. I mean, most halls of residence have set up study hours, so if students don't keep the noise down during the quiet times that have been demarcated for studying, then the Resident Director can give the offending students three verbal warnings.

Student: Yeah, but I don't want the people I live with to know that I've complained about them.

Staff: No problem, it's a completely anonymous, confidential process.

Student: That's good to know. But . . . I mean . . . you're just talking about verbal warnings. What happens if the noisy students just keep ignoring the RD's warnings?

Staff: If they don't heed the warnings, then the RD files a formal complaint with us here at the Accommodation Office, and finally, we have the authority to remove the students.

Student: Oh, okay. I'll have a talk with John to get the ball rolling. Thanks so much for your help!

Listening Test 1 – Task 2:

Teacher: Good afternoon, everyone. In our seminar today, we're going to be discussing an important educational strategy. Since all of you are studying education and are going to be teachers yourselves one day, I'm sure you can appreciate that this is a very worthwhile topic for discussion. It goes without saying that I hope everyone has read the background reading for today! . . . Now, of course, as teachers, you will be able to use a very wide variety of assessment models. So let's look at the pedagogical approach that we are going to discuss today: the student readiness model.

So what do we mean by the student readiness model? Well, as teachers you'll quickly realize that students are individuals, each operating at different levels of ability. For some students, this might mean that they are operating above the average ability level of their contemporaries, while for others . . . um . . . they may be functioning at a level that is below average. Then, too, there are the students who are in what can be called a "comfort zone" . . . these students are learning at the optimum learning level: they are being challenged and learning new things, but yet they don't feel overwhelmed or inundated by the new information.

Okay . . . just to complicate things, we also have to remember that student readiness is not a static entity. In other words, it is constantly changing. Some students will become more confident throughout the semester and will be able to increase their "student readiness." And, unfortunately, other students may fall behind and might slip to a below-average position.

Therefore, the onus falls on us as teachers not only to work out how best to design the curriculum, but also how to structure classroom learning activities that are going to challenge the maximum amount of students. As you will have discovered in your reading for today, the strategy of "question adjustment" can be deployed to help bridge the gap between those students with low readiness and those with high readiness. Now . . . based on the reading, who can explain the concept of "question adjustment"?

Student: Well . . . if I have understood the reading for today correctly, "question adjustment" means that the teacher will ask questions at a variety of different levels of difficulty. There will be some so-called "easy" questions to build the confidence of the students who are less ready. And then, there will also be some really difficult questions, which are supposed to stretch the more capable students, who are the most ready. . . . Did I get that right?

Teacher: Yes, that's perfect! Now can you expand on that point? I'm thinking here about learning materials that can be used in the classroom in order to achieve "question adjustment" . . .

Student: I think I'm with you . . . Are you alluding to what they . . . uh . . . said in the book about posters? That thing about putting up posters in the . . . uh . . . classroom with some of the questions on them, and making sure that each poster has a question of a different level of difficulty?

Teacher: Yes! I can see that you are really very well prepared for today's discussion. Great! Now, let's move on to the area of formal assessment, in other words, quizzes and tests and so on. Now, of course, we should distinguish here between "formal" and "informal." Can anyone explain the difference?

Student: The formal ones are those that count towards the mark or grade for the course. But the informal ones don't.

Teacher: Fantastic! So, as I'm sure you know, the purpose of giving the informal assessment is, again, to help build student confidence. Readiness begets confidence, but conversely, confidence can also help to improve a student's level of readiness.

Listening Test 1 – Task 3:

Skyscrapers vary around the world from city to city, depending on local climate, conditions and, of course, terrain. This is especially true in the world's most heavily populated cities. No recent construction project exemplifies this more clearly than the building of the Hong Kong and Shanghai Bank Corporation (HSBC) in Hong Kong. So, in today's lecture, we're going to have a look at the construction of this particular high-rise building.

First of all, it is interesting to note that a very significant proportion of this structure was prefabricated. In other words, the building was designed so that it had many pre-built parts that were not constructed on site. This prefabrication made the project a truly international effort: The windows were manufactured in Austria, the exterior walls were fabricated in the United States, the toilets and air-conditioning were made in Japan, and many of the other components came from Germany. The prefabrication also had the advantage of making the construction more efficient, as well as minimizing the intrusion and inconvenience to a great many people who continued to work in other buildings near the site.

The HSBC building consists of 47 stories, which is an immense contrast to the twenty-story buildings in its vicinity. In fact, the previous buildings constructed on this site were limited by the soft and often waterlogged ground in the surrounding area. For this reason, the disruption of the ground water supply had to be carefully pondered prior to construction of the HSBC headquarters to ensure that subsidence, and potentially collapse of the structure, could be averted.

So, the basement of the building was made waterproof by constructing massive concrete walls, which were built on site section-by-section. Because the ground was so soft, finding the solid bedrock below was an immense undertaking. This was accomplished by utilizing a dredging apparatus to dig a narrow trench. This trench was kept full of heavy clay during its construction to prevent it from caving in. Then, the trench was dug to a depth of thirty-six meters. More trenches were put in place until the site was completely enclosed on its perimeter. Ultimately, the underground concrete wall that functioned as the basement of the building was the height of a twelve-story building.

Next, the concrete lower floor of the building was constructed so that work above ground could commence. During the next phase of construction, eight giant steel columns, which weighed more than a thousand tons, were erected to support the walls of the structure. In order to support the weight of the building, deep wells were sunk in the bedrock below the building, and then filled with concrete, to anchor each of the eight steel columns.

To provide further support, steel beams stretch across the eight columns at five levels of the structure. Each of these steel beams comprises twin rectangular frames that are, in fact, two stories high. Each steel beam also has hangers, which are used to support the floors. The floors were built simultaneously during the erection of the columns, and the floors were put in place on a temporary basis by using props. So, as soon as each one of the steel beams was in place, the hangers were connected to the completed floors, and the props were moved to the next level . . . to the next floor. Then the process was repeated to enable the construction of each subsequent floor.

Specially-designed cranes then lifted the prefabricated elements of the building into place. Most of the bank's exterior walls are taken up by large panes of window glass. The rest of the building is covered in aluminum panels. The external walls are also prefabricated in an aluminum finish that matched the rest of the building. So, when the external walls were finally lifted into position, they matched seamlessly with the rest of the building.

Listening Test 1 – Task 4:

Meriwether Lewis and William Clark were perhaps the two most famous explorers of the American West. In 1804, the two men began an expedition westward across the area of the United States that was then known as the Louisiana Territory, and along their way, they encountered unknown people and harsh climatic conditions.

Lewis was born on August 18, 1774, in the state of Virginia. Clark was also born in Virginia, although he was four years older than Lewis. The two men met when Lewis joined the local militia, of which Clark was in command. During their experiences in combat, Lewis and Clark made a long-lasting friendship.

Unites States President Thomas Jefferson had been Lewis's neighbor, and when Lewis was a young captain in the army, he received a letter from Jefferson offering him a job in charge of an expedition to explore the Western country.

On February 28, 1803, the United States Congress finally approved the financing for the expedition. At this time, Lewis told President Jefferson that it would be preferable to have a partner for the rigorous journey westward. With Jefferson's permission, Lewis offered the assignment to his friend Clark.

In terms of their backgrounds, abilities, and interests, Lewis and Clark had a great deal in common. They both possessed many traits that would prove to be crucial for such a daunting expedition: they were intelligent, courageous, and loved adventure, and because of their time in the army, they were calm under pressure and able to make important decisions quickly.

The journey that Lewis and Clark made was more than 8,000 miles in length and lasted for nearly two and a half years. The team charted their course by following the Missouri River, and they were responsible for discovering the Northwest Passage. When their expedition had safely concluded, President Jefferson purchased the Louisiana Territory for fifteen million dollars.

Tragically, Lewis died at the age of 35, only three years after the expedition had finished. Clark lived a long and prosperous life in the state of Missouri, where he died peacefully in 1838. It is commonly believed that both men are worthy of laud and praise, providing later generations with an example of heroic patriotism and nationalistic vision.

Listening Test 1 – Task 5:

Teacher: This afternoon, we'll be looking at the function of the human brain. We will also be talking about the way the function, as well as the dysfunction, of the human brain is measured. Now, as you may know, it was in 1929 that electrical activity in the human brain was first discovered. Hans Berger, the German psychiatrist who made the discovery, was despondent to find out, though, that his research was quickly dismissed by many other scientists.

The work of Berger was confirmed three years later, in 1932, when Edgar Adrian, a Briton, clearly demonstrated that the brain, like the heart, is profuse in its electrical activity. Because of Adrian's work, we know that the electrical impulses in the brain, called brain waves, are a mixture of four different frequencies. Here, I should say first of all that by "frequency," we are referring to the number of electrical impulses that occur in the brain per second.

So, as I was saying, there are four types of brain waves. Alpha waves occur in a state of relaxation, while beta waves occur when a person is alert. In addition, delta waves take place during sleep, but they can also occur dysfunctionally when the brain has been severely damaged. Finally, theta waves are of a frequency that is somewhere in between alpha and delta. It seems that the purpose of theta waves is solely to facilitate the combination of the other brain waves.

The whole notion of brain waves, then, feeds into the current controversy about death, especially brain death. Of course, this is considered a very rudimentary, but yet is a very essential question, not only in medicine, but also in law and religion. Some people believe that brain death is characterized by the failure of the cerebral cortex to function. Now, you'll remember that the cerebral cortex is the thinking part of the brain, so under this viewpoint, if a person is no longer physically capable of rational thought, they are considered "brain dead." On the other hand, some say that mere damage to the cerebral cortex is not enough. They assert that brain stem function must also cease before a person can be declared dead, because the cerebral cortex is responsible for other bodily processes.

So, for these myriad reasons, it has become very important to measure brain activity. Now . . . in order to measure brain activity and function, there are various types of equipment, which can perform various types of tests. For instance, we have traditionally used CAT and PET scans for this purpose. Okay, can anybody elucidate . . . between CAT and PET scans?

Student: Well . . . I'll take a stab at it. If I recall correctly, the PET scan works by means of an inert radioactive substance given to a patient, and this allows the doctor to observe the movement of the substance through the brain. As far as the CAT scan, well . . . they are like an X-ray of the brain, which is then displayed on a computer screen.

Teacher: Yes, that right. Now, can anybody talk about the differences between the appearances of CAT and PET scans?

Student: Oh, yeah . . . sorry . . . I should have talked about that, too. The PET scan shows up as one image, and that image will have different colors. And each one of the colors displays the pattern of the brain activity. With the CAT scan . . . that's a cross-section, so, unlike the PET scan, it can be viewed from different angles or positions. And of course, as far as patients are concerned, the CAT is far less invasive because they don't need to ingest a radioactive substance.

Teacher: Great . . . in addition to CAT and PET scans, we now have the MRI scan, which as you know works according to the principles of magnetism. The MRI is perhaps the most indispensable of all of the various scans due to its ability to map the brain in three dimensions.

Listening Test 1 – Task 6:

Antarctica is a mysterious and resilient continent that is often forgotten by virtue of its geographical location. Indeed, the Antarctic is remote and desolate. Nevertheless, an understanding of this continent is critical to our comprehension of the world as a global community. For this reason, the southernmost continent has been the source of a great deal of scientific investigation.

Scientists who have explored this barren land have come from around the world. In 1907, Ernest Shackleton led one of the first expeditions in this area. One of the groups under his supervision was the first to summit Mount Erebus. Shackleton and three other members of his team made several records in the three month period from December 1908 to February 1909. They were the first human beings to travel across the Transantarctic Mountain Range, as well as the first to reach the South Polar Plateau.

In December 1911, Roald Amundsen, a Norwegian explorer, was the first to reach the geographic South Pole, having journeyed via the Bay of Whales and the Axel Heiberg Glacier. Richard Evelyn Byrd also led several explorations of the Antarctic by air throughout the 1930s and 1940s. He then implemented land transport and conducted biological and geographical studies. Later, on October 31, 1956, an expedition led by Rear Admiral George Dufek of the United States Navy successfully landed an airplane on the continent.

In addition, much notable recent research has come from America and Great Britain. The British Antarctic Survey, sponsored by the Natural Environment Research Council of the United Kingdom, and the United States Antarctic Resource Center, a collaboration of the United States Geological Survey Mapping Division and the National Science Foundation, are currently forerunners in the burgeoning field of research in this area.

This corpus of research has resulted in an abundance of factual data on the Antarctic. For example, we now know that more than ninety-nine percent of the land is completely covered by snow and ice, making Antarctica the coldest continent on the planet. This inhospitable climate has, not surprisingly, brought about the adaptation of a plethora of plants and biological organisms present on the continent. An investigation into the sedimentary geological formations provides testimony to the process of adaptation. Sediments recovered from the bottom of Antarctic lakes, as well as bacteria discovered in ice, have revealed the history of climate change over the past 10,000 years. Containing nearly seventy percent of the world's freshwater supply, Antarctica plays a crucial role in the world's ecosphere. Therefore, the Antarctic is also a key factor in current global climate change. On its surface, it possesses a four kilometer thick ice sheet. This mammoth sheet of ice atrophies because of year-round melting at its base, as well as the loss of ice due to the formation of icebergs. However, the ice sheet is also perpetually replenished by snowfall and frost.

At present, two methodologies are employed to measure the size of the ice sheet. The first is the accumulation method, by which the difference between the loss of ice and the accumulation of new precipitation is calculated. The second technique, known as the direct measurement approach, involves the use of satellites to determine whether the ice sheet is growing thicker. Yet, unfortunately, both methods have a rather large potential for error.

The measurement of the ice sheet is of paramount importance because scientists fear that the melting of a large amount of the ice sheet may occur as a result of global warming. Some of them believe that human beings are directly responsible for any potential ecological catastrophe, pointing to their excessive reliance on fossil fuels for domestic use and transportation. On the other hand, some assert that natural causes also have a part to play in the debacle, especially volcanic eruptions. While there are some uncertainties about the phenomenon of global warming, it is indisputable that the current rate of sea level change is unprecedented.

The melting of the ice sheet, of course, inevitably leads to a dramatic rise in sea levels. Recent research suggests that the greenhouse effect, a term used to describe the causes of global warming, has already caused the oceans to raise ten to twenty centimeters. Computer models are currently being used to predict the probability of further sea level increases, but many scientists fear that even with a small sea level rise, certain nations and cultures that have existed for millennia will be destroyed.

TOEFL Listening Practice Test 2

This listening practice test contains 6 parts (34 total questions). You have 60 minutes to complete all six parts of this listening test.

Listening Test 2 – Task 1:

1. What reason did the student give for being late to class?

    A. She has an earlier class that finishes late.

    B. She works part-time in the library.

    C. She takes her child to the day care center.

    D. Her little girl is ill.

2. Why does the teacher say this? "Is it a quick question?"

    A. To express disapproval about the student's tardiness

    B. To scold the student for not making an appointment

    C. To encourage to student to speak about her problem in detail

    D. To point out that he doesn't have much time to talk

3. What does the student mean when she says this? "I'm not really with you."

   A. She doesn't understand what the teacher has implied.

   B. She doesn't want to continue the discussion.

   C. She doesn't want to leave with the teacher.

   D. She disagrees with the teacher's previous statement.

4. Based upon the teacher's comments, what can be inferred about some of the other students in the class?

   A. They have agreed to help this student with her problem.

   B. They may be unhappy about the current situation.

   C. They agree with the solution the teacher has proposed.

   D. They don't like having refresher sessions.

5. What solution did the teacher and student agree upon?

   A. The student should make alternative child care arrangements.

   B. The student will attend the class at a different time of day.

   C. The student needs to discuss her problem with another student.

   D. The student should get class notes from another student.

Listening Test 2 – Task 2:

6. What is the main idea of this lecture?

    A. The development of music in the Western world

    B. The history of music during the last two centuries

    C. The professional biography of Beethoven

    D. The variety of symphonic forms

7. Based on the lecture, what can be inferred about polyphonic music?

    A. Its style has remained static over the centuries.

    B. It is the musical preference of many people.

    C. It is the compulsory musical style for national anthems.

    D. It has a more varied sound than monophonic music.

8. Which of the following statements best describes the opera?

    A. It helped Greek drama to develop.

    B. The Italian opera was indistinguishable from other styles of the opera.

    C. It started to include oratorios during the sixteenth century.

D. It began to include a variety of musical instruments during the sixteenth century.

9. What does the professor say about the German-born composers?

    A. They enabled the development of concertos.

    B. Their music had an international style.

    C. They disliked the use of the violin.

    D. Their worked ended in the seventeenth century.

10. How does the professor support her statement that "Beethoven links the classical and romantic periods"?

    A. With a personal opinion about Beethoven

    B. With explanations and definitions

    C. With examples from the classical period

    D. With biographical information about the composer

11. According to the lecture, which of the following points is true?

    A. Monophonic music is one of the earliest types of music.

    B. Polyphonic music consists of one sound or voice.

    C. The opera developed during the eighteenth century.

    D. Bach and Handel were active during the seventeenth century.

Listening Test 2 – Task 3:

12. What is the main idea of the lecture?

    A. The impact of nutrition on health

    B. The dangers of excessive dieting

    C. New advice about protein consumption

    D. Nutritional requirements for teenagers

13. What does the professor imply when he says this? "Carbohydrates seem to have gotten bad press lately."

    A. Carbohydrates are bad for the health.

    B. Carbohydrate consumption results in low energy levels.

    C. Recent public debate has emphasized the negative aspects of carbohydrates.

    D. Carbohydrates help to repair damage to the body.

14. What does the professor state about fruit and vegetables?

    A. Each person should consume an apple daily.

    B. It is important to eat at least five portions daily.

    C. Medical practitioners give different advice about fruit and vegetables.

    D. Most people have difficulty consuming the correct amount of fruit and vegetables.

15. Which one of the following warnings about protein consumption does the professor specifically mention?

   A. A person should be careful to eat a sufficient amount of dairy products.

   B. Because it is a better protein source, red meat should be eaten instead of rich cheese.

   C. The consumption of fish should be increased.

   D. Every individual should monitor the amount of fatty protein he or she consumes.

16. How does the professor support his statement about food additives?

   A. By giving reasons for their dangers

   B. By describing the public's general preference

   C. By discussing a specific medical case study

   D. By providing a personal anecdote

17. Which one of the following statements is correct according to the discussion?

   A. Healthy nutrition means that food is consumed from five major groups.

   B. Sugar consumption need not be restricted.

C. Processed and convenience foods may damage the health.

D. Energy requirements remain constant regardless of a person's age

Listening Test 2 – Task 4:

18. What usually happens when cells divide?

    A. the abnormal growth of organs

    B. tumors begin to grow

    C. more cells form without order

    D. the human body is kept healthy

19. What is metastasis?

    A. the growth of cancer in a cell

    B. the growth of cancer outside a cell

    C. the growth of cancer inside a tumor

    D. the spread of cancer from a tumor

20. What is the biggest cause of cancer in America?

    A. poor nutrition

    B. overexposure to the sun

    C. smoking

    D. being underweight

21. How does cancer compare to other diseases?

    A. It is the first leading cause of death.

    B. It is the second leading cause of death.

C. It is the third leading cause of death.

D. It is the fourth leading cause of death.

22. How many American women will eventually develop cancer?

   A. one-fourth

   B. one-third

   C. 13%

   D. 30%

23. How many American men develop cancer during their lifetimes?

   A. one-fourth

   B. one-half

   C. 5%

   D. 15%

Listening Test 2 – Task 5:

24. What does the student mean when he gives this response?

    "I know them by heart."

    A. He hardly knows the information required.

    B. He has memorized his ID and password.

    C. He understands that the ID and password are necessary.

    D. He has written down the ID and password.

25. According to the computer assistant, what mistake do students often make when creating a new password?

    A. They create invalid messages.

    B. They forget to include capital letters.

    C. They forget to include certain required characters.

    D. They try to use forbidden symbols.

26. What is the computer assistant implying when he says this? "Well . . . it's all explained on page 39 of your student handbook, so . . ."

    A. The student has misunderstood the instructions in the handbook.

    B. The explanation contained in the student handbook is unclear.

    C. The student should have read the instructions in the handbook.

    D. She has become impatient with the student.

27. How does the computer assistant attempt to solve the student's problem?

   A. By giving a detailed step-by-step explanation

   B. By telling the student to read the handbook more carefully

   C. By describing common problems all students face

   D. By referring the student to another university department

28. What is the outcome at the end of this conversation?

   A. The student has to go to Computer Services to obtain a new password.

   B. The student manages to log in to the computer system successfully.

   C. The computer assistant changes the student's password.

   D. The student finally remembers his computer ID.

Listening Test 2 – Task 6:

29.. What does NTSB stand for?

    A. National Transportation Security Board

    B. National Transportation Safety Board

    C. National Transportation Security Bureau

    D. National Transportation Safety Bureau

30. When did the NTSB's affiliation with the Department of Transportation end?

    A. 1967

    B. 1975

    C. 1977

    D. 1979

31. What purpose does the NTSB serve regarding aircraft accidents?

    A. It investigates whether the accident occurred on or near a highway.

    B. It calculates the number of fatalities.

    C. It determines the cause of the accident.

    D. It implements recommendations.

32. Which one of the following is not the work of the NTSB?

    A. Enforcing safety recommendations

    B. Investigating major transportation accidents

    C. Aiming to prevent future accidents

    D. Preparing a list of most-wanted improvements

33. What is one benefit of the implementation of NTSB recommendations?

    A. Saving lives due to the reduced occurrence of accidents

    B. Increasing the amount of tax on medical care for accident victims

    C. Increasing wages due to injury and death

    D. Supporting crash victims

34. How does the economy indirectly improve when NTSB recommendations are made law?

    A. Less tax money needs to be spent on emergency medical care.

    B. Crash victims claim for lost wages.

    C. There are fewer lawsuits for wrongful death.

    D. There is more government funding for crash investigation.

Listening Test 2 – Answer Key

1. C
2. D
3. A
4. B
5. B
6. A
7. D
8. C
9. B
10. B
11. A
12. A
13. C
14. B
15. D
16. A
17. C

18. D
19. D
20. C
21. B
22. B
23. B
24. B
25. D
26. C
27. A
28. B
29. B
30. B
31. C
32. A
33. A
34. A

Listening Test 2 – Answers and Explanations

1) The correct answer is C. The student stated: "I have a little girl . . . she's four . . . and I have to drop her off at the day care center before class."

2) The correct answer is D. The professor implies that he is in a hurry when he says: "Is it a quick question?"

3) The correct answer is A. "I'm not with you" means: I don't understand what you have said.

4) The correct answer is B. The professor states: "You have to get another one of the students to repeat all of that information to you, and that's where the inconvenience comes in for them." Because the other students are inconvenienced, they are probably unhappy about the situation.

5) The correct answer is B. The professor states: "There is a student in the same course, but her class meets at 2:00. She can't come then because she just got a part-time job, so if it's okay with you, maybe the two of you could change places. She could come to the 9:00 and you could take her place in the 2:00 session."

6) The correct answer is A. The professor mentions the main topic of the lecture in her first sentence: "the tradition of music in the Western world." She goes on to describe the changes in musical style from the thirteenth century to the eighteenth century.

7) The correct answer is D. The professor states: "As polyphony developed, musical traditions began to change, and this meant that music began to rely on a greater range of voices." In other words, polyphonic music has a more varied sound because it has a greater range of voices.

8) The correct answer is C. The professor states: "Especially during the end of the sixteenth century, there was an attempt to return to the tradition of Greek drama. This had a particular influence on the opera. As a result, the opera expanded to include oratorios."

9) The correct answer is B. The professor states: "Since many of the German-born composers studied abroad, baroque music was regarded to possess an international style."

10) The correct answer is B. The professor states: Beethoven "added deeper texture – by this I mean the depth and breadth of different types of instrumental sound – as well as aesthetics – and here by aesthetics we are talking about the beauty of the music itself, in other words, the sheer pleasure or enjoyment that a person can receive from listening to a truly beautifully composed piece of music. For these reasons, the music of Beethoven is commonly regarded as establishing the end of the classical period."

11) The correct answer is A. At the beginning of the lecture, the professor states: "Prior to the thirteenth century, chant was the dominant mode of music. Notably, chanting was a monophonic form of music."

12) The correct answer is A. At the beginning of the discussion, the professor states: "So today, we're going to talk about good nutrition. Now, everybody knows that good nutrition is essential for good health."

13) The correct answer is C. The professor states: "Although carbohydrates seem to have gotten bad press lately, in fact, they are an essential part of healthy nutrition." "Gotten bad press" means that something has received negative comments from the public or news media.

14) The correct answer is B. The professor states: "Most medical practitioners in the United States now recommend a minimum consumption of five portions of fruit or vegetables every day."

15) The correct answer is D. The professor states: "Lean protein is better than fatty protein, so it's best to limit the consumption of red meat, rich cheeses, and cream."

16) The correct answer is A. The professor states: "Packaged food often contains chemicals, such as additives to enhance the color of the food or

preservatives that give the food a longer life. These chemicals aren't good for the health for two reasons."

17) The correct answer is C. The professor states that packed and processed foods "aren't natural and may perhaps be linked to disease in the long term. In addition, they may block the body's ability to absorb energy and nutrients from food."

18) The correct answer is D. The human body is usually kept healthy when cells divide. The speaker states: "All internal organs of the body consist of cells, which normally divide to produce more cells when the body requires them."

19) The correct answer is D. Metastasis is the spread of cancer from a tumor. The lecturer explains that "in some cases the cancer from the original tumor spreads. The spread of cancer in this way is called metastasis."

20) The correct answer is C. Smoking is the biggest cause of cancer in America. The speaker comments that "smoking is the largest single cause of death from cancer in the United States."

21) The correct answer is B. Cancer is the second leading cause of death. The speaker states that "cancer is now the second leading cause of death in the United States."

22) The correct answer is B. One-third of American women will eventually develop cancer. The speaker says: "One-third of all American women and half of all American men will develop some form of cancer during their lifetimes."

23) The correct answer is B. One-half of American men will develop cancer. The speaker says: "One-third of all American women and half of all American men will develop some form of cancer during their lifetimes."

24) The correct answer is B. The student states: "I know them by heart." This expression means that a person has memorized something.

25) The correct answer is D. The computer assistant states: "That's a common problem students experience. You see, there are certain characters and symbols that you can't use in your password."

26) The correct answer is C. The student previously stated that he wasn't aware of the rules. When the computer assistant states: "Well . . . it's all explained on page 39 of your student handbook," she is implying that it was the student's responsibility to have read the rules.

27) The correct answer is A. The computer assistant gives these steps: "You just need to press control-alt-delete, and the system will ask you to change your password. So then you should type in a new one that doesn't

have one of those forbidden characters in it. Of course, I'm sure I don't need to remind you to choose a password that you can remember."

28) The correct answer is B. At the end of the conversation, the student says "I'm in." This means that he has managed to log in to the computer system.

29) The correct answer is B. NTSB stands for National Transportation Safety Board. The speaker begins by stating that "the National Transportation Safety Board, also known as the NTSB, was established on April 1, 1967."

30) The correct answer is B. The NTSB's affiliation with the Department of Transportation ended in 1975. The speaker states: "Under the Independent Safety Board Act of 1975, however, this organizational relationship was ultimately severed, meaning that the NTSB is no longer affiliated with the Department of Transportation or any of its related agencies."

31) The correct answer is C. The NTSB determines the causes of aircraft accidents. The speaker says: "The United States Congress charges the NTSB with determining the cause of every passenger aircraft accident in the United States."

32) The correct answer is A. Enforcing safety recommendations is not the work of the NTSB. The lecturer comments that "even though the NTSB issues these recommendations, it does not enforce them, resulting in its reputation for fairness and impartiality."

33) The correct answer is A. One benefit of the implementation of NTSB recommendations is that lives are saved due to the reduced occurrence of accidents. The speaker points out that the NTSB has "an extremely positive effect in terms of saving lives."

34) The correct answer is A. The speaker states that "these laws have also indirectly improved the economy since they reduce the amount of tax dollars spent on emergency medical care for crash victims. "

Listening Test 2 – Texts

Listening Test 2 – Task 1:

Student: Hi Professor Johnson. Have you got a minute?

Teacher: Uh . . . well . . . I have a class in about five minutes. Is it a quick question, or would you like to schedule an appointment during my office hour on Friday?

Student: Oh . . . well . . . I'm afraid I can't come on Friday because I work in the library part-time. Anyway, hopefully it won't take too long.

Teacher: Okay. What's up?

Student: Well, you've probably noticed that I'm usually late for your 9:00 class.

Teacher: Yes, of course I have, and to be honest, I'm glad you've dropped in to talk about that.

Student: The thing is . . . you know . . . I'm a mature student . . . and I'm a single parent too . . . I have a little girl . . . she's four . . . and I have to drop her off at the day care center before class . . . Well . . . the day care center only opens at 9:00, so that's why I'm always late, because I have to go there first.

Teacher: Well, have you talked to the people who run the day care center? Would it be possible to drop your little girl off a bit early? I mean, could one of their members of staff be available before 9:00?

Student: No, I'm afraid not. I already asked them that, and the person in charge told me that because of their license, they can't open before 9:00. It's something to do with the regulations of running a day care center, and it just can't be changed.

Teacher: Oh, I see. That's too bad. It must be inconvenient for you, but you know it's also causing inconvenience . . . in a way . . . to the other students in the 9:00 class.

Student: Uh . . . I'm not really with you.

Teacher: Well, what I'm getting at is . . . your persistent tardiness . . . it's become a little disruptive. I mean . . . I'm sure you've noticed that we usually start off the class with questions and a "refresher" session from the previous class, so you miss all of that information. And then, of course, you have to get another one of the students to repeat all of that information to you, and that's where the inconvenience comes in for them, in a way.

Student: Well . . . what do you think I can do? I mean . . . I'm sorry, but it's just not going to be possible for me to be there on time.

Teacher: Okay . . . look . . . there is a student in the same course, but that class meets at 2:00. She can't come then because she just got a part-time job, so if it's okay with you, maybe the two of you could change places. She could come to the 9:00 and you could take her place in the 2:00 session? What do you think?

Student: Oh, yes! That would be great. It would really solve my problem.

Teacher: Great! Okay . . . well . . . leave it with me . . . I'll talk to the other student and see if she'll agree to joining the 9:00 group. Then, I'll send you an email to let you know. Is that okay?

Student: That's great. Thanks a lot, Professor Johnson. I really appreciate it! See you later.

Listening Test 2 – Task 2:

The tradition of music in the western world – in other words, music as we know it today – originated in the genre of chanting. Prior to the thirteenth century, chant was the dominant mode of music. Notably, chanting was a monophonic form of music. Now, monophonic, let's have a look at that word . . . "mono" is from a Greek word. It means one thing alone or by itself. "Phonic" is also Greek in origin – and it means sound. So, monophonic music consists of only one sound or voice that combines various notes in a series.

Polyphonic music appeared in the fifteen century during the early Renaissance period. In contrast to monophonic music, polyphonic music consists of more than one voice or instrument, and it combines the notes from the different sources together simultaneously. As polyphony developed, musical traditions began to change, and this meant that music began to rely on a greater range of voices. And really this was a big range . . . um . . . I mean . . . from the very high to the very low. This kind of polyphonic musical influence is also present in the national anthems that emerged in various countries during this era.

Next, let's have a look at the sixteenth century. Particularly, here, especially during the end of the sixteenth century, there was an attempt to return to the tradition of Greek drama. This had a particular influence on the opera. As a result, the opera expanded to include oratorios, which are extended sung musical compositions on a particular subject. This phenomenon was especially pronounced in the Italian opera, and so, the opera, in turn, dominated the musical style of the early seventeenth century.

The seventeenth century also witnessed the proliferation of musical instruments. Musical compositions and arrangements for keyboard instruments, such as the piano and organ, thrived during this period. Music for the orchestra, arrangements like sinfonias and concertos, also began to take off at this time.

Now, next, let's look at the the eighteenth century. The eighteenth century was marked by the development of baroque music. Stringed instruments, particularly the violin, were predominant throughout this epoch. Since many of the German-born composers studied abroad, baroque music was regarded to possess an international style. Other forms of classical music, especially the symphony, also developed during this century.

Okay, so, eighteenth century music – many people believe this anyway – was dominated by two German-born geniuses: Bach and Handel. These two composers wrote music in almost every genre, including opera and oratorio music. Handel, of course, studied in both Italy and England, bearing out the point I made earlier about the international flavor of the musical compositions of this century. Bach, while similar in many ways to Handel, is perhaps best known for his liturgical – and by this I mean religious – music. Some music history scholars point out that Bach's work is significant historically, too, since it shows the pervasive impact of the Reformation on the musical style of this century.

Finally, then, no lecture on musical genre would be complete without a discussion of Beethoven. Beethoven really was a remarkable and versatile musician. He contributed to almost every style of music during his era, including piano, strings, and symphonies, and he expanded the form of the symphony to include greater orchestration.

Beethoven is often seen as the crucial link between the classical and romantic periods. He added deeper texture – by this I mean the depth and breadth of different types of instrumental sound – as well as aesthetics – and here by aesthetics we are talking about the beauty of the music itself, in other words, the sheer pleasure or enjoyment that a person can receive from listening to a truly beautifully composed piece of music. For these reasons, the music of Beethoven is commonly regarded as establishing the end of the classical period.

Listening Test 2 – Task 3:

Teacher: So today, we're going to talk about good nutrition. Now, everybody knows that good nutrition is essential for good health. Indeed, a healthy diet can help a person to maintain a good body weight, promote mental wellbeing, and even reduce the risk of disease. So, first of all today, we are going to look at the answer to the question: What does healthy nutrition consist of?

Well, really, a healthy diet should include food from four major groups. These four groups are carbohydrate, fruit, vegetables, and protein. The first of the four groups, carbohydrate, includes food like potatoes, bread, and cereals. Although carbohydrates seem to have gotten bad press lately, in fact, they are an essential part of healthy nutrition, because . . . well . . . importantly, they provide the building blocks for supplying energy to the body.

The second and third food groups are fruit and vegetables – although some people would just include these as one group. This may seem easy to understand at first blush, but it is worth pointing out here that good nutrition depends on eating a variety of fruit and vegetables. While the old adage "An apple a day keeps the doctor away" may appear to be sound advice, eating the same fruit or vegetables daily . . . um. . . it's not the best advice in reality. The amount of fruit and vegetables . . . now that's also important to bear in mind. Most medical practitioners in the United States now recommend a minimum consumption of five portions of fruit or vegetables every day.

Protein includes food such as meat and fish, as well as dairy products, like milk and cheese. However, lean protein is better than fatty protein, so it's best to limit the consumption of red meat, rich cheeses, and cream. In addition to keeping an eye on fat intake, the amount of sugar a person eats also needs to be moderated.

Now, the question I want to ask as this point is, do you think that it's better to give up sugar completely in order to achieve optimal health?

Student: I don't think a person should try to forego sweets altogether. It's just that consuming too much sugar is often connected to health problems later in life, like Type II diabetes, so I think the thing is, to try to be careful not to eat too much sugar.

Teacher: Yes, that's right. Like the old saying goes: Everything in moderation.

Next, let's move on and look at the health risks posed by processed or convenience food. Of course, fresh food is far better than packaged or processed food. Packaged food often contains chemicals, such as additives to enhance the color of the food or preservatives that give the food a longer life. These chemicals aren't good for the health for two reasons. First of all, they aren't natural and may perhaps be linked to disease in the long term. And in addition, they may block the body's ability to absorb energy and nutrients from food, with nutrients being the essential vitamins and minerals that are required for healthy bodily function.

Finally, let's have a look at nutritional requirements for adults. Here, by "adult," I mean people from 19 to 50 years of age. Now, let's think about this for a moment. Do you think that energy requirements . . . I mean in terms of the number of calories consumed . . . do you think they are higher for teenagers or adults?

Student: Isn't it true that teenagers would probably need more calories than adults? Because, I mean, teenagers are still in their growing phase, aren't they?

Teacher: Yes, great answer! It's absolutely true that compared to children and teenagers, energy requirements for adults are lower for both men and women. Nevertheless – and this is extremely important – the nutritional requirements for vitamins and minerals for adults remain unchanged compared to teenage years. Of course, I should also mention that adult women experience increased nutritional requirements during pregnancy.

Listening Test 2 – Task 4:

Cancer, a group of more than 100 different types of disease, occurs when cells in the body begin to divide abnormally and continue dividing and forming more cells without control or order. Importantly, all internal organs of the body consist of cells, which normally divide to produce more cells when the body requires them. This is a natural, orderly process that keeps human beings healthy.

However, if a cell divides when it is not necessary, a large growth called a tumor can form. These tumors can usually be removed, and in many cases, they do not come back. Unfortunately, in some cases the cancer from the original tumor spreads. The spread of cancer in this way is called metastasis.

There are some factors which are known to increase the risk of cancer. Smoking is the largest single cause of death from cancer in the United States. One-third of the deaths from cancer each year are related to smoking, making tobacco use the most preventable cause of death in this country.

Choice of food can also be linked to cancer. Research shows that there is a link between high-fat food and certain cancers, and being seriously overweight is also a cancer risk. Cancer risk can therefore be reduced by cutting down on fatty food and eating generous amounts of fruit and vegetables.

Skin cancer is the most common type of cancer for both men and women. Repeated exposure to the sun, through sunbathing for example, greatly increases a person's chance of developing this kind of cancer. As a general rule, it is usually best to avoid the sun during midday and early afternoon, but when this is not possible, one should be sure to use protective sun-blocking creams.

Cancer is now the second leading cause of death in the United States. One-third of all American women and half of all American men will develop some form of cancer during their lifetimes. Yet, millions of people have been successfully treated for cancer. The sooner cancer is found and treatment starts, the better one's chances are for successfully treating the cancer and living a long and healthy life.

Listening Test 2 – Task 5:

Student: Hi. I was wondering if you could help me?

Staff: Let's see . . . what's your question?

Student: Well, I just registered for classes on Thursday last week, and I received my computer ID and password yesterday, but when I try to log in to the computer system on campus, I keep on getting an error message.

Staff: Oh . . . okay . . . do you remember what the message says?

Student: No . . . unfortunately, I don't . . . It just gives me a message saying that I can't log in.

Staff: Have you got your ID and password with you?

Student: No, but I know them by heart.

Staff: Okay, great! Why don't you try to log on to this computer right here, and we'll see what happens.

Student: Okay. Here goes . . . There . . . There's the message I keep getting. Do you see it? It says something about invalid password characters.

Staff: Right . . . that's a common problem students experience. You see, there are certain characters and symbols that you can't use in your password . . . things like the slash, the question mark, and the number sign, for example.

Student: Oh . . . well . . . why's that?

Staff: Those kinds of symbols are forbidden for passwords because the computer uses them in mathematical calculations. Have you tried to use any symbol like that in your password?

Student: Yeah . . . I have . . . but I didn't realize that I wasn't supposed to.

Staff: Well . . . it's all explained on page 39 of your student handbook . . . so . . .

Student: Oh . . . right . . . I get it . . . It was my responsibility to read that, but you know, I was just so tired after I had registered that I didn't really have the energy to read the handbook all the way through.

Staff: No problem. Actually, we're used to that . . . I mean we hear that a lot.

Student: So, what can we do now to solve the problem?

Staff: It should be pretty easy to solve, actually. You just need to press control-alt-delete, and the system will ask you to change your password. So then you should type in a new one that doesn't have one of those forbidden characters in it. If course, I'm sure I don't need to remind you to choose a password that you can remember!

Student: Sure! Can I try to change it now and see what happens?

Staff: Yes, please do. That's a good idea.

Student: Okay . . . let me try this . . . okay . . . I put the new one in now. The system seems to have accepted it. Can I try to log in again?

Staff: Yes, go ahead.

Student: Okay . . . there's my ID . . . now . . . the new password . . . . great! I'm in! Thanks so much for your help!

Listening Test 2 – Task 6:

The National Transportation Safety Board, also known as the NTSB, was established on April 1, 1967. The NTSB was an independent body, but initially received financial and administrative support from the Department of Transportation. Under the Independent Safety Board Act of 1975, however, this organizational relationship was ultimately severed, meaning that the NTSB is no longer affiliated with the Department of Transportation or any of its related agencies.

The United States Congress charges the NTSB with determining the cause of every passenger aircraft accident in the United States, as well as with investigating major accidents involving other types of transportation, such as those occurring on highways, railways, waterways, or pipelines. As a result of its investigations, the NTSB issues important recommendations, which are aimed at preventing the occurrence of future accidents and improving passenger safety.

The National Transportation Safety Board has issued in excess of 12,000 recommendations to more than 2,200 recipients. In addition, it has highlighted important issues on a list of most-wanted safety improvements. Even though the NTSB issues these recommendations, it does not enforce them, resulting in its reputation for fairness and impartiality. This has allowed for a vast improvement in transportation safety because more than 82 percent of the organizations receiving NTSB recommendations have adopted their safety measures.

Many benefits accrue to society and the economy when NTSB recommendations are implemented. For example, enforcement of seat belt laws has led to a significant reduction in fatal injuries. While of course having an extremely positive effect in terms of saving lives, these laws have also indirectly improved the economy since they reduce the amount of tax dollars spent on emergency medical care for crash victims, as well as lowering the amount of lost wages due to injury or death.

TOEFL Listening Practice Test 3

This listening practice test contains 6 parts (34 total questions). You have 60 minutes to complete all six parts of this listening test.

Listening Test 3 – Task 1:

1. Which question is central to the investigation of human choice?

    A. Can human beings make choices that will alter their futures?

    B. Are human beings capable of making good decisions?

    C. Why do human beings have to choose?

    D. What are the artistic viewpoints on nature?

2. What is epistemology?

    A. the study of being

    B. the study of knowledge

    C. the study of decision making

    D. the study of cosmic forces

3. What aspects of human personality are investigated?

    A. emotional

    B. spiritual

    C. physiological

    D. both A and B

4. What is the fourth problem area of the philosophy of human nature?

   A. unity

   B. complexity

   C. personality

   D. human choice

5. The course studies the writings of which philosopher?

   A. Platinus

   B. Plato

   C. Phaedrus

   D. Pluton

Listening Test 3 – Task 2:

6. Why did the student miss class?

   A. She misunderstood the policy on attendance.

   B. She didn't know what time the class met.

   C. She has a medical problem.

   D. She was late and was too embarrassed to attend.

7. Why does the teacher say this?

   "I said that a student needed to see me as soon as possible following an absence."

   A. To imply that the student has waited too long to discuss the situation.

   B. To remind the student of the exact nature of the attendance policy.

   C. To clarify the reasons for the establishment of the policy on absences.

   D. To answer a question that the student has posed.

8. What does the teacher mean when he says this?

   "We will have to give you more leeway."

   A. The teacher is saying that now the absence is more serious.

   B. The teacher will be more flexible with the student.

- C. The teacher is saying that there is no excuse for the absence.
- D. The teacher is saying that the university will consider the case carefully.

9. Based upon the teacher's tone of voice at the beginning of the discussion, what can be inferred about his attitude?
    - A. He is completely happy to help the student in any way possible.
    - B. He is upset about the policy that the university has established.
    - C. He realized that the attendance policy is confusing for students.
    - D. He feels a little bit annoyed that the student did not come to see him sooner.

10. What solution did the teacher suggest to the student?
    - A. To complete an additional assignment in lieu of the lecture.
    - B. To arrange for another student to share his or her notes.
    - C. To provide the student with copies of the PowerPoint slides from the lecture.
    - D. To offer the student extra advice for the final examination.

Listening Test 3 – Task 3:

11. What is the main idea of this lecture?

    A. To give the background to genetic engineering and discuss recent legal claims in this area

    B. To give the background to genetic engineering and discuss its current controversies

    C. To describe the genetic engineering of plants in detail

    D. To describe the historical development of the genetic engineering of animals

12. What example does the professor give when discussing the earliest forms of genetic engineering?

    A. cereals and fruit

    B. insects

    C. the super-tomato

    D. sheep

13. What is the professor implying when he says this? "I don't need to write that on the board, do I?"

    A. The genetic characteristics should be obvious.

    B. This idea will be discussed in more detail later.

C. The students should already be aware of this term.

D. This idea will not be included on the examination.

14. How does the professor support his discussion of gene splicing?

    A. By identifying a common trend

    B. By drawing on statistical data

    C. By discussing the conclusions reached by a particular scientist

    D. By giving specific examples

15. What is Factor 9?

    A. a birth defect

    B. a biological agent that causes excessive bleeding

    C. an area of Scotland

    D. something that helps blood to clot

16. Which of the following groups of statements give the best summary of the lecture?

    A. (i) Genetic engineering has a relatively recent scientific background.

    (ii) The super-tomato can grow in severely cold conditions.

    (iii) DNA is the essential part of every living cell.

B. (i) Genetic engineering has a relatively recent scientific background.

(i) The process of genetic engineering involves gene splicing of part of the DNA chain.

(iii) There have been several ethical and moral debates about genetic engineering recently.

C. (i) DNA is the essential part of every living cell.

(ii) The process of genetic engineering involves gene splicing of part of the DNA chain.

(iii) The super-tomato can grow in severely cold conditions.

D. (i) The process of genetic engineering involves gene splicing of part of the DNA chain.

(ii) The super-tomato can grow in severely cold conditions.

(iii) There have been several ethical and moral debates about genetic engineering recently.

Listening Test 3 – Task 4:

17. What organization occupied the offices that were burglarized?

    A. the Democracy Nationalism Committee

    B. the Democratic National Committee

    C. the Democratic National Caucus

    D. the Democratic National Council

18. Who initially discovered the burglary?

    A. the ringleader

    B. the police

    C. the security guard

    D. five men in suits

19. What did the burglars have in their pockets?

    A. one-hundred-dollar bills

    B. burglary tools

    C. tape

    D. keys

20. What did the police investigation confirm?

    A. The burglars were part of a professional ring.

    B. Several items were stolen.

C. The burglars had removed telephone equipment.

D. The men worked for Gordon Liddy

21. What is CREEP?

A. Committee for Reconciliation of the Presidency

B. Committee for the Re-election of the President

C. Committee for the Resurgence of the Presidency

D. Council for the Re-election of the President

22. What happened to the men who committed the burglary?

A. They went on to the highest branches of government.

B. They became FBI investigators.

C. They managed to commit a cover-up operation.

D. They were incarcerated for their crimes.

Listening Test 3 – Task 5:

23. What is the main idea of the discussion?

    A. reasons for the decrease in teenage smoking

    B. reasons for teenage experimental smoking

    C. recent trends in teenage smoking

    D. teenage smoking and peer pressure

24. Apart from peer pressure, what reason is given for the increase in teenage smoking?

    A. the decrease in the price of cigarettes

    B. feelings of alienation from within the family

    C. lawsuits against tobacco companies

    D. disadvantaged home life

25. What does the professor mean when he says this? "You hit the nail on the head!"

    A. The student's remarks were very apt.

    B. The student has managed to keep the discussion going.

    C. The student has touched on a sensitive subject.

    D. The student needs to focus on the main points.

26. From the discussion, what can be inferred about lawsuits against tobacco companies?

   A. They affected affluent families more profoundly than poor families.

   B. They affected teenagers more than adults.

   C. Cigarette companies had to increase their prices because of the expense of hiring lawyers.

   D. Cigarette companies had to reduce their prices to increase demand.

27. What is the outcome of teenage experimental smoking?

   A. Most experimental smokers do not manage to quit.

   B. It causes an increase in cigarette prices.

   C. It can lead to drug addiction.

   D. It can be overcome through logical steps.

28. How does the professor support his comments about experimental smoking?

   A. By giving an example

   B. By citing a medical authority

   C. By giving statistical data

   D. By mentioning troubles teenagers encounter generally

Listening Test 3 – Task 6:

29. When did the first official Olympic Games take place?

    A. 393 AD

    B. 776 BC

    C. 1896 AD

    D. 1393 AD

30. How many events did the Pentathlon include?

    A. 3

    B. 5

    C. 7

    D. 9

31. Who was not allowed to compete in the ancient Olympic Games?

    A. Chariot racers

    B. Greek-born men

    C. Women

    D. Pentathletes

32. What is the IOC?

    A. International Olympic Committee

    B. International Official City

C. International Olympic City

D. International Olympic Council

33. What happens during "The Parade of Nations"?

    A. athletes begin to compete

    B. athletes march around the stadium

    C. athletes take the Olympic Oath

    D. the committee oversees the participants

34. What is the purpose of the Olympic Games?

    A. To oversee athletes from various countries

    B. To make money on a national level

    C. To promote friendship among the nations

    D. To support their host countries

Listening Test 3 – Answer Key

1. A
2. B
3. C
4. A
5. B
6. C
7. A
8. B
9. D
10. C
11. B
12. A
13. C
14. D
15. D
16. B
17. B
18. C

19. A
20. A
21. B
22. D
23. C
24. B
25. A
26. D
27. A
28. C
29. C
31. B
31. C
32. A
33. B
34. C

Listening Test 3 – Answers and Explanations

1) The correct answer is A. The following question is central to the investigation of human choice: "Can human beings make choices that will alter their futures? The speaker states: "The first problem area, human choice, asks whether human beings can really make decisions that can change their futures."

2) The correct answer is B. Epistemology is the study of knowledge. The speaker explains that "epistemology means the study of knowledge."

3) The correct answer is C. The emotional and spiritual aspects of human personality are investigated. The speaker states: "The third key issue, human personality, emphasizes aspects of human life that are beyond mental processes. It takes a look at emotional, spiritual, and communal elements."

4) The correct answer is A. Unity is the fourth problem area of the philosophy of human nature The speaker comments that "the fourth problem, the unity of the human being, explores the first three areas more fully and asks whether there is any unifying basis for human choice, thought, and personality."

5) The correct answer is B. The course studies the writings of the philosopher Plato. The speaker concludes by stating that: "the works of

Plato and Aristotle are generally regarded as the foundation for this subject."

6) The correct answer is C. The student stated: "my medical condition makes me feel quite tired."

7) The correct answer is A. The teacher emphasizes the phrase "as soon as possible," thereby implying that too much time has passed.

8) The correct answer is B. The teacher goes on to talk about giving the student more time for her homework. "Leeway" means flexibility with policies or rules.

9) The correct answer is D. You can understand the annoyance from the teacher's tone of voice, especially when he says: "Of course, all of the information conveyed in class is important! And to be honest, I'm quite surprised that you're asking about it only now!"

10) The correct answer is C. The teacher states: "Why don't I just give you a copy of my PowerPoint slides for the lecture that you missed. Would that be helpful?"

11) The correct answer is B. At the beginning of the lecture, the professor states: "In the lecture for today, we're going to take a look at a hotly-debated and contentious topic: genetic engineering. So, first of all, we'll go into a little bit of background information about this topic. Then, we'll move

on to consider the nuts and bolts . . . by that I mean the basics of . . . the genetic aspects of genetic engineering. And finally, we'll have a look at why this topic has become such a thorny issue recently."

12) The correct answer is A. The professor states: "It's probably no surprise to you that scientists have been conducting genetic engineering on plants for quite a few years now . . . things like cereals and fruit, for example."

13) The correct answer is C. The professor implies that there is no need to write the term on the board because the students should already know this term.

14) The correct answer is D. After bringing up the idea of gene splicing, the professor mentions the super-tomato and Factor 9 as examples of this phenomenon.

15) The correct answer is D. The professor states: "If someone who doesn't have Factor 9 is inflicted with a deep cut or gash and they start bleeding . . . because that person's blood doesn't clot in the normal way, they could suffer extensive blood loss."

16) The correct answer is B. The professor mentions the three main ideas stated in choice B. The other ideas mentioned in choices A, C, and D are stated in the lecture, but they are specific points, not main ideas.

17) The correct answer is B. The Democratic National Committee occupied the offices that were burglarized. The speaker states: "The break-in took place on June 17 of that year when five men [. . .] entered the office of the headquarters of the Democratic National Committee."

18) The correct answer is C. The security guard initially discovered the burglary. The speaker comments that the burglars "were caught by a security guard after they had surreptitiously entered the office."

19) The correct answer is A. The burglars had one-hundred-dollar bills in their pockets. The speaker states that "they had filled their pockets with sequentially numbered one-hundred-dollar bills."

20) The correct answer is A. The police investigation confirmed that the burglars were part of a professional ring. The speaker comments that "the police later confirmed that the men were part of a professional ring."

21) The correct answer is B. CREEP is Committee for the Re-election of the President. The speaker explains that " CREEP [. . .] stands for the Committee for the Re-election of the President. "

22) The correct answer is D. The speaker states that "the men who had entered the highest branches of the American government to serve and protect the people went to prison instead."

23) The correct answer is C. At the beginning of the discussion, the professor states: "In today's class, we're going to talk about a worrying sociological problem, that of teenage smoking. Although the trends show that smoking by adults has been declining steadily over the past few decades, the percentage of teenagers who smoke only started to drop in the late 1990s."

24) The correct answer is B. The student states: "With the increase in the use of things like the internet and with a lot of parents working long hours, maybe kids feel a bit . . . sort of . . . alienated."

25) The correct answer is A. The expression "You hit the nail on the head" means that someone has just said an apt or appropriate remark.

26) The correct answer is D. After describing the lawsuits, the professor states: "paradoxically, these teenagers were from well-off families and could have afforded to pay the higher prices, yet contrary to these market forces, the price of tobacco products was reduced during this time."

27) The correct answer is A. The student states that she thinks most experimental smokers won't manage to quit. Then the professor says: "Yes, that's absolutely right."

28) The correct answer is C. At the end of the discussion, the professor gives this data: "The statistics bear this out. A recent study on high school

students showed that 56 percent of the students who smoked predicted that they would not still be smokers five years after graduation, but when the data was gathered five years later, only 31 percent of them had actually quit smoking."

29) The correct answer is C. The first official Olympic Games took place in 1896 AD. The speaker states: "The first official Olympic Games took place in Athens in 1896."

30) The correct answer is B. The Pentathlon included five events. The speaker explains that "perhaps the most grueling sport was the Pentathlon, an event which included five parts."

31) The correct answer is C. Women were not allowed to compete in the ancient Olympic Games. The speaker comments that "women were forbidden to compete or even to enter the stadium during the ancient games."

32) The correct answer is A. The IOC is the International Olympic Committee. The speaker states that "the Olympic Games are governed and organized on an international level by the International Olympic Committee, known as the IOC."

33) The correct answer is B. The speaker states that during the "parade of nations [. . .] the athletes march around the stadium to represent their host country."

34) The correct answer is C. The purpose of the Olympic Games is to promote friendship among the nations. The speaker states: "The games [. . .] are said to promote friendship and understanding among nations."

Listening Test 3 – Texts

Listening Test 3 – Task 1:

The study of the philosophy of human nature is often regarded as an investigation into the meaning of life. This subject usually deals with four key problem areas: human choice, human thought, human personality, and the unity of the human being. A consideration of these four problem areas can also include scientific and artistic viewpoints on the nature of human life.

The first problem area, human choice, asks whether human beings can really make decisions that can change their futures. Conversely, it investigates to what extent the individual's future is fixed and pre-determined by cosmic forces outside the control of human beings.

In the second problem area, human thought, epistemology is considered. Epistemology means the study of knowledge; it should not be confused with ontology, the study of being or existence.

The third key issue, human personality, emphasizes aspects of human life that are beyond mental processes. It takes a look at emotional, spiritual, and communal elements. Importantly, the study of the communal aspect focuses on community and communication, rather than on government or the philosophy of the state.

Finally, the fourth problem, the unity of the human being, explores the first three areas more fully and asks whether there is any unifying basis for human choice, thought, and personality. In other words, while the human is an inherently complex being, there must be a unity or wholeness underlying these complications.

The study of the philosophy of human nature should enable an individual to contemplate more deeply vital human issues, including an engagement with political, cultural, and social debates. Not surprisingly, the works of Plato and Aristotle are generally regarded as the foundation for this subject.

Listening Test 3 – Task 2:

Student: Hi Professor Emerson. I know you're busy, but could I speak with you for a couple of seconds.

Teacher: No problem. Have a seat.

Student: The thing is, you know, I was absent three weeks ago, and I was wondering if I missed anything important.

Teacher: Yes, of course, all of the information conveyed in class is important! And to be honest, I'm quite surprised that you're asking about it only now.

Student: Sorry, I'm not following you.

Teacher: What I'm getting at is . . . I'm sure you remember at the beginning of each semester when I mention the policy on absences. I said then that a student needed to see me as soon as possible following an absence.

Student: Oh . . . yeah . . . I see what you mean. I just realized today, though, when you were talking about the test that's coming up next week . . . I was worried about the session I missed, in case any of that information is on the exam.

Teacher: I can't reveal any information about what's going to be covered on the end-of-semester test. But I can tell you that it is a comprehensive test . . . Well . . . three weeks have passed since you missed the class . . . That's quite a long time, don't you think?

Student: Yeah . . . I'm a little bit embarrassed about it . . . That's why I hesitated to see you about the problem . . . Actually, I've just been diagnosed with diabetes. I've kind of been struggling the past couple of weeks to pay attention in class, because my medical condition makes me feel quite tired.

Teacher: Well . . . when a student has a medical condition, it is considered to be an extenuating circumstance, so we can excuse your absence. We will also have to give you more leeway . . . about your homework and so on.

Student: Oh . . . that's great news, because as I said, I've been finding it really difficult to concentrate.

Teacher: Well, as you know, I usually tell absent students to copy the lecture notes from a friend. But in your case, why don't I just give you a copy of my PowerPoint slides for the lecture that you missed. Would that be helpful?

Student: That would be great! Will any of the information from that lecture be on the test?

Teacher: As I said, I really can't give precise details about the final exam. But I would emphasize again, that it's a comprehensive test. So anything we have talked about in class can be included on the final exam.

Student: Okay, so I'll just review everything for the final test. Did I miss any homework?

Teacher: Actually, there was a 300 word personal response piece that's due next Tuesday. But if you can give me a note from your doctor as evidence of your medical condition, I can give you a two-week extension.

Student: No problem. I can bring the doctor's note to our next class. Is that okay?

Teacher: That would be fine. Now . . . here are copies of the PowerPoint slides . . . Is there anything else I can help you with?

Student: No, that's all. Thanks so much for your help.

Teacher: No problem at all. See you in class next week.

Listening Test 3 – Task 3:

Okay everybody, I think we should probably get started. In the lecture for today, we're going to take a look at a hotly-debated and contentious topic: genetic engineering. So, first of all, we'll go into a little bit of background information about this topic. Then, we'll move on to consider the nuts and bolts . . . by that I mean the basics of . . . the genetic aspects of genetic engineering. And finally, we'll have a look at why this topic has become such a thorny issue recently.

Okay . . . Genetic engineering . . . now as biology students you'll know that this term refers to the process of re-programing the genetic materials that dictate how a plant or animal behaves. And it's probably no surprise to you that scientists have been conducting genetic engineering on plants for quite a few years now . . . things like cereals and fruit, for example. Now, this has been done to produce better fruit . . . to grow fruit . . . or even vegetables, for that matter . . . outside of their normal season, and to make other plants, especially cereal crops, more resistant to damage from insects and disease. So, of course, the next question is . . . we all may be aware of the basic idea behind genetic engineering, but what exactly . . . um . . . I mean . . . how is genetic engineering carried out on a genetic or biological level specifically and precisely? . . . That's the question we'll look at next.

Well, as we all know, the genetic characteristics of any organism are present in its DNA . . . DNA . . . I don't need to write that on the board, do I? . . . Oh, okay . . . So DNA . . . deoxyribonucelic acid . . . is the genetic material found in each and every living cell. These form a genetic code and are formed from long molecules . . . like chains . . . and these DNA chains consist of four separate components called nucleotides . . . okay . . . that's a difficult term. . . I'd better put that one on the board . . . nucleotides . . .

It's the order of these nucleotides on the DNA chain that determines the reproductive information for the cells. In other words, the specific genetic information along any point of this DNA chain will determine a particular genetic trait. By way of example . . . in the case of human beings . . . a particular portion of your DNA might show your doctor if you are susceptible to a disease, like cancer or Alzheimer's disease.

So, then, in order to carry out what is known as genetic engineering, gene splicing needs to be done first. Gene splicing . . . this describes the process whereby a small part of the DNA chain for one characteristic of one organism is cut out of the DNA chain for that organism and inserted into the DNA chain of another organism from another species.

And this has produced results like the "super-tomato." Now, the "super-tomato" was genetically engineered by inserting some DNA from cold-water fish . . . the particular gene for resistance to cold temperatures was isolated on the DNA chain of the fish and was removed. This cold-resistant gene was then re-inserted into an ordinary tomato plant . . . and lo and behold . . . we've now got tomato plants than can grow . . . or dare I say . . . even thrive . . . in cold weather conditions.

Another experiment, that was even more notorious that the "super-tomato," was that of Factor 9. Factor 9 is a genetic agent that is responsible for the clotting of blood. So if some people have a birth defect and are born without Factor 9 in their DNA chain, it would be really easy for them to bleed to death in the event of an accident. I mean, let's say for example, someone who doesn't have Factor 9 is inflicted with a deep cut or gash and they start bleeding . . . because that person's blood doesn't clot in the normal way, they could suffer extensive blood loss, or even lose their life, very quickly. So some scientists in Scotland several years ago found a way to grow and extract Factor 9 from sheep . . . and then reinsert that sheep gene into people who were at risk of severe bleeding because they didn't have the Factor 9 gene.

Anyway, probably by now, you've realized why this area has become so controversial lately. As animal rights groups have come into more prominence socially and politically, and people are more and more aware of the suffering of animals, many people question whether using animals in this way is medically reasonable . . . indeed whether it is even ethical or moral.

Listening Test 3 – Task 4:

The burglary at the Watergate building in 1972 is one of the most famous crimes ever recorded in America. The break-in took place on June 17 of that year when five men, impeccably dressed in suits and ties, were caught by a security guard after they had surreptitiously entered the office of the headquarters of the Democratic National Committee.

The security guard reported that the burglary was apparently planned. He told the police that a piece of tape had been placed over a lock in a door leading to the headquarters in order to keep the door open. The police also discovered that the men were wearing gloves and that they had filled their pockets with sequentially numbered one-hundred-dollar bills. Most importantly, the men were carrying burglary tools.

Even though a ringleader was not named, the police later confirmed that the men were part of a professional ring. The police reported that nothing was stolen, and it was evident that the men had chosen the offices for their break-in because they were searching for specific documents. It is also known that the men were attempting to repair a bug, which is a secret telephone listening device, that they had installed three weeks before the break-in.

The Watergate burglary had many aspects, but at its center was President Richard Nixon. The lawbreaking reached to various branches of the United States government and included administrators within the White House. It later emerged that the five men who conducted the burglary worked under the direction of G. Gordon Liddy, who was President Nixon's finance counsel. Liddy was in charge of an organization known as CREEP, which stands for the Committee for the Re-election of the President.

Throughout the investigation of the burglary, government officials denied involvement in the crime. An extensive cover-up operation followed in an attempt to conceal those who were involved in planning the break-in. Yet, this subterfuge failed when the FBI investigated the one-hundred-dollar bills that were found in the pockets of the burglars. After making inquiries, the FBI discovered that this money originated from the CREEP organization, thereby confirming governmental involvement. In the end, men who had entered the highest branches of the American government to serve and protect the people went to prison instead.

Listening Test 3 – Task 5:

Teacher: In today's class, we're going to talk about a worrying sociological problem, that of teenage smoking. Although the trends show that smoking by adults has been declining steadily over the past few decades, the percentage of teenagers who smoke only started to drop in the late 1990s. In fact, the current statistics on this are really quite alarming because, at present, the rate of teenagers who smoke is nearly 50 greater than the rate for adult smokers. So, my first question is this: what reasons can you give for these trends?

Student: Well, could it be that teenagers are more prone to pressure from their friends, you know, peer pressure, and so of course they want to fit in with their social group and smoking is one way to do that.

Teacher: Yes, good answer! Peer pressure is really one of the biggest reasons why teens smoke. But, you know, peer pressure has always existed from time immemorial. Can you think of any other reasons . . . um . . . I mean reasons that are specifically connected with current social and cultural phenomena?

Student: Oh, yeah, I see what you're getting at. You know, with the increase in the use of things like the internet and with a lot of parents working long hours, maybe kids feel a bit . . . sort of . . . alienated . . . is that the right word? I mean, like if the kid is by himself a lot maybe he's just going to feel alone and not connected to anybody else but his friends and then of course he's more susceptible to fall into the trap of smoking because of peer pressure.

Teacher: Yes, exactly! You hit the nail on the head! In fact, recent research shows that the rise in teenage smoking in the 1990s primarily took place in the youth from more affluent families – you know, their parents were working and earning good incomes, so of course the children were not from disadvantaged homes as some sociologists would like us to believe . . . quite the opposite . . . the most striking and precipitous rise was in teenagers with the most financially advantageous backgrounds.

And we know that because of various law suits against the major tobacco companies, the price of cigarettes actually declined sharply in the early 1990s, which of course added fuel to the fire that was already burning in this area socially. What I mean is, paradoxically, these teenagers were from well-off families and could have afforded to pay the higher prices, yet contrary to these market forces, the price of tobacco products was reduced during this time.

Okay . . . so from this we can surmise that price doesn't really appear to be a factor in smoking by teens. Probably, this is because teenagers often view themselves as "experimental smokers." Now that's an interesting term . . . "experimental smokers" . . . what to you think it means or implies?

Student: Well, it means they see their own smoking behavior as an experiment obviously. So what that implies . . . I suppose . . . is that these kids think they are just trying it out, so they aren't necessarily . . . actually . . . going to do it . . . I mean smoke . . . for their lifetime . . . They maybe just view it as something they can try and then stop doing it later.

Teacher: Yes, I couldn't have said it better myself! Okay . . . So, the next logical question is: Do you think that most of these teenagers . . . these experimental smokers . . . will eventually manage to stop smoking?

Student: Personally, I think that's highly unlikely. I mean, I've heard that quitting smoking is an extremely difficult thing to do . . . I've heard it can even be tougher than beating drug addiction . . . because the nicotine in cigarettes is very highly addictive itself.

Teacher: Yes, that's absolutely right. And, again, the statistics bear this out. A recent study on high school students showed that 56 percent of the students who smoked predicted that they would not still be smokers five years after graduation. But when the data was gathered five years later, only 31 percent of them had actually quit smoking.

Listening Test 3 – Task 6:

The Olympic Games have a long and rich history. The first official Olympic Games took place in Athens in 1896, although experts point out that there is evidence of ancient Olympic Games taking place as early as 776 BC. Athletes in these ancient games competed on the plains of the Greek city of Olympia. The ancient Olympic Games were part of a religious festival and continued for nearly twelve centuries, until banned by Byzantine Emperor Theodosius in 393 AD.

The ancient Olympic Games consisted of several athletic events. Perhaps the most grueling sport was the Pentathlon, an event which included five parts: running, jumping, wrestling, boxing, and the discus throw. The ancient games also included equestrian events, such as horse and chariot racing.

While women were forbidden to compete or even to enter the stadium during the ancient games, many female athletes compete in various events in today's Olympic Games. In addition, although only Greek-born men were allowed to compete in the ancient games, men and women from all over the world come to compete and represent their countries in the modern Olympic Games.

Nowadays, the Olympic Games are governed and organized on an international level by the International Olympic Committee, known as the IOC. The IOC establishes the program of events and chooses the city in which the games are to be held. On the national level, each country that sends athletes to the games has a National Olympic Committee that oversees the participation of the athletes for their countries.

The opening ceremony of the games is held in a stadium in a major city. After the parade of nations, in which the athletes march around the stadium to represent their host country, the athletes take the Olympic Oath. The games, which are said to promote friendship and understanding among nations, then officially begin.

www.ingramcontent.com/pod-product-compliance
Lightning Source LLC
Chambersburg PA
CBHW081351080526
44588CB00016B/2457